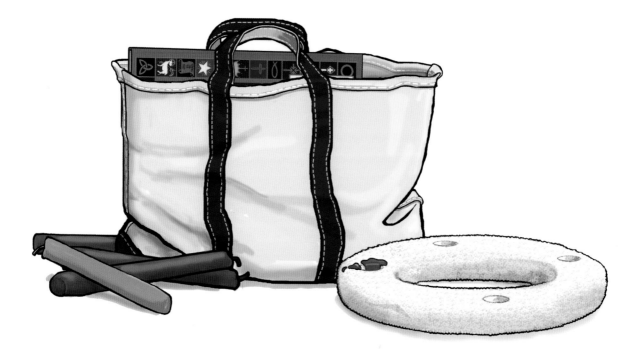

Mouse Tales
Things Hoped For

Advent, Christmas, and Epiphany

Written by Ruth L. Boling
Illustrated by Tracey Dahle Carrier

WJK WESTMINSTER
JOHN KNOX PRESS
LOUISVILLE • KENTUCKY

Text © 2005 Ruth L. Boling
Illustrations © 2005 Tracey Dahle Carrier

Scripture quotations, unless otherwise indicated, are from the New Revised Standard Version of the Bible, copyright © 1989 by the Division of Christian Education of the National Council of the Churches of Christ in the U.S.A., and used by permission.

Book design by Tracey Dahle Carrier and Teri Vinson
Cover design by Teri Vinson
Cover illustration: Tracey Dahle Carrier

First edition
Published by Westminster John Knox Press
Louisville, Kentucky

This book is printed on acid-free paper that meets the American National Standards Institute Z39.48 standard. ♾

PRINTED IN HONG KONG

05 06 07 08 09 10 11 12 13 14 – 10 9 8 7 6 5 4 3 2 1

Library of Congress Cataloging-in-Publication Data

Boling, Ruth L.
    Mouse Tales–things hoped for : Advent, Christmas, and Epiphany / by Ruth L. Boling ;
illustrated by Tracey D. Carrier.
        p. cm.
    Summary: A congregation of mice works together to prepare their church and their hearts for Advent, Christmas, and Epiphany, and welcomes a new family into the fold.
     ISBN 0-664-22705-8
    [1. Christian life–Fiction. 2. Advent–Fiction. 3. Christmas–Fiction. 4. Epiphany–Fiction. 5. Churches–Fiction.
6. Mice–Fiction.] I. Carrier, Tracey Dahle, ill. II. Title

PZ7.B6359118Mo 2005
[Fic]–dc22   2004054948

Dedication

For my mother,
Jean Eleanore Gade Boling,
who brought hope to life.

~R. L. B.

For my dear sister Jennifer,
who shares the childhood memories
that have wiggled their way
into these illustrations.

~T. D. C.

Message from the Author

If you're familiar with the phrase "quiet as a church mouse," be forewarned: the church mice in these stories are anything but quiet. Inquisitive, kindhearted, mischievous, stubborn, they engage one another in tasks that give meaning to everyday life, taking their bearings from lively Sunday School debates and traditional services of worship.

Individual story themes correlate to the liturgical seasons of Advent, Christmas, Epiphany, and Ordinary Time. The stories are especially appropriate over the four-month period from December through March, but can be enjoyed any time of the year.

The book's subtitle comes from Hebrews 11:1–"Now faith is the assurance of *things hoped for,* the presence of things not seen." Christian hope derives from our experience of God's activity in the world, and calls us to participate in it. Sometimes we make a mess of things, but somewhere in the beautiful tangle of human action and interaction we encounter God, we experience grace, we are moved by the Spirit. Life in all its complexity yields hope, thrives on hope, requires hope.

The church mice of Hillsborough–whether they realize it or not–participate significantly in God's work. An underlying hopefulness propels them along their way, and the result of all their adventures, mishaps, joys, and entanglements is more hope. In a fear-driven, post-9/11 world where authentic hope is hard to come by, I pray that children and other readers will find in these stories a reservoir of hope whose wellspring is Jesus the Christ, who is called Emmanuel, which means God-with-us.

Ruth L. Boling

Table of Contents

The Church of the Least of These takes its name from God's promise to Jeremia

hat all shall "know me, from the least of them to the greatest."

(Jeremiah 31:34; see also Luke 9:48 and Matthew 25:40

Snapshots

Rose Noel: Forward thinking and athletic, Rose loves a challenge of any kind. Having a twin sister makes her good at teamwork. She is lively, outgoing, and unswervingly loyal.

Lily Noel: Lily notices the world in astonishing detail. She makes art wherever she goes, using whatever she finds. Her talent is a source of pride among her church friends.

Frank Treadwell: Count on Frank to blurt out what everyone else is thinking. Sunday School teachers, beware. Frank will challenge any statement that doesn't make plain sense.

Max Wynne: Max spins small ideas into grand schemes. He likes the limelight. If there were such a thing as a Christian Super Hero, he would want to be one.

Ernest Graves: With Frank and Max around, Ernest is the odd one out. He retaliates by behaving well in church and quoting Bible verses. His motto is Romans 3:23.

Amber Everly: Jesus, Church, and the Bible are new to Amber. She asks question after question that no one else would think to ask. Her Sunday outfits create a stir.

Harold (Hal) Louis: Not long ago Hal belonged to the Youth Group. Now he's the Youth Adviser. He says, "Praise the Lord!" about once every five minutes, and he means it.

Gloria Kelsey: Miss Gloria teaches the middle elementary Sunday School class. She is young and fun and always running late. She lets the children do most of the talking.

The Rev. Claire Fixler: Pastor Claire focuses on action. Younger and less sure of herself than Theo, Claire works harder than she really needs to. She livens things up.

The Rev. Theophilus Hartiswell: Pastor Theo views everything in the light of God's will and Christ's love. He thinks before speaking or acting. If he's befuddled, he'll say so.

Papa Jordan: His ancestors founded the town and the church, and he himself is very old. Just how old, nobody knows. He takes long walks every morning, using his cane.

Mrs. Constance Grumble: A widow living alone, Mrs. Grumble is devoted to protecting the church from spills and messes. She watches the children like a hawk.

Things Hoped For

Rose Noel sat up, stretched, and blinked away the fuzziness that separates sleep from wakefulness. Sliding off the bed, she leapt over the scarves, mittens, and woolen socks she'd piled up on the floor the night before, and raced to the window. Gray skies all day yesterday had promised an overnight snowfall, but the hard ground and tangled tree branches remained bare.

"Rats," she said, and turned toward Lily, her twin sister, who was smiling softly in her sleep. "Wake up!" Rose jiggled her by the shoulders. "You asked me to get you up, so get up, OK?"

Lily finally stirred. "Did it snow?"

Rose shook her head, no.

"It snowed in my dream."

"Oh?" Rose seldom remembered her own dreams. She turned away, straightened her sheets and tugged at the corners of her comforter.

"You and I were sitting in church," said Lily, "and everything was normal until the choir stood up to sing. Mrs. Handelbach played a few chords on the organ, and just as the choir shaped their mouths into Os, it started snowing inside the sanctuary."

Rose fluffed up her pillow and smiled.

"Lacy snow–the kind where you can see whole clusters of snowflakes land on your mittens. Only we weren't wearing mittens, and we didn't feel cold."

After washing up, Rose put on one of the matching blue velour dresses that hung side by side in the twins' closet. Lily watched, propped up on her elbows, while Rose twirled exactly once in front of the mirror. "So majestic," Lily observed, "a perfect color for Advent. No wonder they call it royal blue." Then she tilted her gaze toward the ceiling and furrowed her brow into a crosshatch of ridges. Rose waited to hear the rest of Lily's dream.

"A layer of snow covered the continued. "It looked like a cake Mrs. Mousseau's hat completely filled Doughnut Head." Rose giggled. "Each sprig was trimmed in white. The ushers wore ice down the aisle with the offering plates."

pulpit Bible," Lily decoration. The brim of up with snow, and we called her of evergreen on the Advent wreath skates, and they glided up and

"Good morning, girls." The twins' mother smiled at them from the doorway. "Your waffles are ready, so be quick. If you're out the door in fifteen minutes, you'll be on time for Sunday School."

"Impossible," muttered Lily, looking down at her bare feet and rumpled pajamas, and then over at Rose, who was making the final adjustments to her hair bow.

"Speak for yourself," retorted Rose.

"Oh, girls, remember to bring these for the Clothing Exchange Box." Mrs. Noel held up a plump brown shopping bag. They had filled it yesterday with clothing the twins had outgrown.

"Oh, Mom," Lily protested, "can't I just . . ."

"No you can't, Lily, honey, we've already discussed this. They're too small for you, but for some other little girl they'll be a dream come true, just in time for Christmas."

Lily flashed Rose a look of, first, desperation, then misery, and then righteous indignation, but Rose was unmoved. She stepped coolly into her church shoes and buckled them. Taking up the shopping bag, she left for the kitchen, without a word.

❄❄❄❄❄

Being a few minutes late to Sunday School didn't bother Lily as much as it did Rose. The girls tumbled in the door and over to the coatrack, creating their usual flurry as they hung up scarves, coats, pocketbooks, muffs, and spare gloves. Their classmates, three boys, were already seated: Frank Treadwell, Max Wynne, and Ernest Graves.

"Hi, guys," Rose grinned around the table. Rose's cheerful voice told Lily that something–maybe just the five minutes of fresh air walking to church–had staved off her sister's bad mood before it could take hold.

"We're not late after all," said Lily.

"No, not very," replied Ernest, pushing up his left sleeve and checking his enormously complicated wristwatch. "Your arrival at two minutes and twenty-four seconds past nine was, technically speaking, late, but not exceedingly so."

The girls were used to Ernest's persnickety comments and ignored him. They got along better with Frank and Max. What a pair! The practical and outspoken Frank stood nearly a head taller than his best friend, Max, who was a big dreamer and an even bigger talker. Lily looked at them now. Frank appeared to be his usual, matter-of-fact self, but something about Max was definitely not right. He looked shrunken, and about ready to disappear into his drab, brown sweater. Frank stared at Max. Max stared at the floor. Neither of them spoke.

"I had a fantastic dream last night," Lily announced, when suddenly the door flew open. In rushed Gloria Kelsey, their Sunday School teacher.

"I'm sorry to keep you waiting," she said, flashing a bright smile around the room. She reached into her tote bag and lifted out a Styrofoam ring, three blue candles, and one pink one. Then came lesson books, a Bible, construction paper, pencils, scissors, markers, and a box of safety matches.

Lily and Rose clapped in delight when they saw the Advent wreath. Frank and Ernest leaned over for a closer look. But Max slumped in his chair and let out a low moan.

On the way to the water cooler after class, Lily overheard Frank talking to Max. "What's the matter?" Frank asked.

"Nothing, and I don't want to talk about it," said Max.

Just then, Rose walked by swinging a shopping bag over one arm. Lily bolted after her, and the girls raced down the hallway. They squared off in front of the Clothing Exchange Box, each tugging on one handle of the bag.

"Let go!" Lily shouted.

"You let go."

"We can't throw these away."

"We're not. We're giving them away."

Suddenly the bag tore, and the clothes spilled out. Rose was quicker than Lily. She scooped everything up and dumped it all into the box. Turning her back to her sister, Rose wadded up the torn shopping bag and dribbled it like a soccer ball down the hall to the trash can.

Lily sank to her knees in front of the box and pulled out dresses, one by one. She traced a collar line, held a satin sleeve to her cheek, caressed a row of buttons, and buried her face in a faded nightgown. She gazed for an especially long time at a purple jumper with a wrinkled bow—last year's Advent dress—worn on the day she and Rose had lit the candles at the beginning of worship. She was scrunching up her face to keep from crying when the sound of snickering reached her ears.

That Rose! Winning wasn't enough for her. She had to rub it in. Lily spun around to confront her tormenter, but it wasn't Rose. It was only the boys. Frank and Max, to be exact. She didn't care if they teased her. Boys were always tormenting girls. She laughed out loud with relief.

"Show-off!" growled Max. "You only got picked because you're a girl and a twin," he said. "Well, maybe someone else wanted a turn, and maybe someone else doesn't want to see that old dress of yours, or watch you cry while you think about the greatest day of your life. A dream come true for you just might be somebody else's nightmare. Did you ever think of that?"

Lily blinked and frowned. Then she remembered. "Hey, Max, you were in my dream, too," she said, excitedly. "It was snowing in the sanctuary, and you were tilting your head back, catching snowflakes on your tongue. I forgot you were there until right this second. Can you imagine that?"

"Ummmmm, yes," Max replied. "I think . . . I can imagine that."

CLOTHING EXCHANGE

2
R-E-P-E-N-T

In Max's opinion, the Sunday School Advent wreath was just a stupid ring from the craft store. For the second Sunday in a row, when Miss Gloria asked him to light it, Max said no. But the real Advent wreath was a different story. It was made of evergreens and rested high up on a wrought iron wreath stand in the sanctuary. Every year, four lucky families were chosen to light the candles on the four Sundays of Advent. One very lucky family would light the Christ candle on Christmas Eve.

The Noel twins had a turn last year. Why them, and not me? Max wondered. Surely he would do an excellent job. The truth is, Max wanted a turn more than anything in the world. He dreamed of standing beside the evergreen wreath and gazing out over the congregation. Before lighting the candles he would recite the Bible readings, by heart. After lighting them he would offer the Prayer of the Day, also by heart. Max couldn't explain this deep longing of his. Lighting the Advent candles would make him a church celebrity, but there was more to it than fame.

Ernest finally volunteered to light the puny little Sunday School candles, and then Miss Gloria walked over to the chalkboard. "Today's lesson is on John the Baptist. He preached about getting ready for Jesus. He told everyone to repent." R-E-P-E-N-T, she wrote. Max froze. Did Miss Gloria know? Was today's lesson aimed at him? Had Pastor Theo told her what happened two Fridays ago at the potluck dinner?

❄ ❄ ❄ ❄ ❄

Actually, the dinner had been OK. Max ate macaroni and cheese, potato chips, carrots, and three desserts. But after dinner, when they moved into the sanctuary for the Hanging of

16

the Greens, everything unraveled. Max had helped Mr. Chipman clip branches of balsam into short sprigs just the right length for twisting into the long ropes used for decoration. He'd held the ladder steady while Mr. McNutt climbed up and draped the choir loft railing in elegant swags. He'd been supervising all five of the Blythe children—Billy, Tillie, Millie, Lillie, and Jilly—as they trimmed the tree, when Pastor Theo entered the sanctuary, lugging the heavy wreath stand. Max saw his opportunity and sidled over.

"Want some help?" he asked. Pastor Theo looked relieved, and tilted the wreath stand sideways. "Ready, set, lift!" In order to keep his end level with Pastor Theo's, Max hoisted it up to his chest, like a weight lifter with a barbell. They cut a wide path as they walked together to the chancel area. The wreath stand took a wild dive on its way back down but landed safely on the carpeted floor. Thunk!

"Thank you, Max." He and Pastor Theo shook hands. Then Pastor Theo slipped the circle of evergreens over the frame and placed the taper candles in their holders.

"Nice Advent wreath," said Max.

Pastor Theo was straightening the candles and didn't seem to hear him. Max decided to wait until he finished. Then Max would have his full attention. He planned to shuffle shyly from one foot to the other, stammer, and finally wonder out loud whether his lifelong dream of lighting the Advent candles might come true this year. . . . But Pastor Theo was having some trouble. He could only get three candles standing straight at one time. When he tried for the fourth, he would knock the first three all akimbo.

After several minutes of this, Mrs. Constance Grumble stepped in. Hoo boy, thought Max. Mrs. Grumble was the reason children didn't nibble crackers in the sanctuary, or drink red punch in the parlor. Mrs. Grumble was known for putting herself in charge and getting things done, her way. Clucking her tongue and shaking her head, she had all four candles standing at attention in no time. Then she took the Christ candle from Pastor Theo and lowered it easily into the center. "There," she said, and she gave his arm a pat. Brushing the evergreen needles from her skirt, she walked off.

Pastor Theo's mouth dropped open and his hands fell to his sides. He looked as if he'd just been robbed, and he looked smaller than Max remembered, maybe because he wasn't wearing his Sunday robe.

All of sudden, Max laughed. Oh no! He clamped his mouth shut, but the laughter came snorting out his nose instead. He pretended the snort was a sneeze, and tried faking another sneeze, but that only gave him the hiccups. He wound up in the church kitchen with Hal Louis, the Youth Group adviser. They tried three different cures before his hiccups went away. By the time Max got back to the sanctuary, Pastor Theo was gone.

❄ ❄ ❄ ❄ ❄

An elbow jab from Frank brought Max to his feet for the closing prayer. Tendrils of smoke from the Sunday School Advent candles swirled and vanished. R-E-P-E-N-T was still the only word printed on the chalkboard. Max gulped. He hadn't paid attention to the lesson. Now it was too late, and there was no going back.

The ten-minute break between Sunday School and

worship felt more like an hour. Frank kept pestering Max to explain his strange behavior. Ernest felt Max's forehead and said he must have a fever. *Throng, throng, throng.* At the sound of the chimes Max bolted into the sanctuary and sat down with his older brother, Royal, and his parents, in their usual spot in the third pew from the front. The last note of the last chime left pure silence in its wake. Worship had begun.

Max wished whoever was going to light the candles would get on with it. He glanced over his shoulder, but all he saw was an old man with a cane blocking the whole aisle and slowing everything down. Oh, great! The congregation began whispering. Max twisted around for a better look. The old man's gnarled cane looked familiar.

"Papa Jordan?" Max asked Royal. Royal nodded. Papa Jordan was said to be the oldest living mouse in Hillsborough. "What's he doing?" Royal shrugged. Planting his cane firmly before each step, Papa Jordan walked all the way into the chancel, turned left, and continued up to the Advent wreath.

He faced the congregation, took a piece of paper out of his vest pocket, put it back in, and took off his glasses instead. "As a young child I dreamed of doing this." Papa Jordan tapped the evergreen wreath lightly. The congregation fell silent. "You can't imagine what this means to me today." He put his glasses back on, took the paper back out, and read,

> Rejoice, O Zion,
> and be ye glad, O Jerusalem,
> for the Lord your God comes.

Leaning his cane against the pulpit, he took the brass candlelighter from an usher. Holding it with two hands, he turned, aimed, and lit the first candle on the first try, but he couldn't quite reach the wick of the second candle. Max held his breath. Letting go with one hand, Papa Jordan stretched a little bit higher. Clank!! Brass clattered against wrought iron, and the congregation gasped as the candlelighter fell into the evergreen boughs. The usher yanked it out and pinched out the flame before anything caught fire.

Papa Jordan took off his glasses and wiped his brow with a handkerchief. Then he reached for his cane. "I was afraid something like this might happen," he said, looking out over the rows of anxious faces. "Won't one of you children light the other candle for me? You there, up front." He pointed his glasses directly at Max!

Max rose to his feet slowly. He looked from Papa Jordan to the Advent wreath and back again. Finally, he spoke. "No. I mean, no thank you. Papa Jordan, sir, you've waited a long time for your turn. Please . . . try again."

Leaning into his cane, Papa Jordan shook his head. "I can't."

"Just try," came a voice from the back. "We'll wait."

Someone else urged, "One more try, Papa Jordan."

"You can do it," said another.

Cries of "We're with you," and "Try again, Papa Jordan," came from all directions.

Papa Jordan looked over at Pastor Theo, who nodded in agreement. Setting his cane aside and putting his glasses back on, Papa Jordan grasped the candlelighter with both hands and waited while the usher relit the wick. Taking a deep breath, he aimed, reached, and—in one gracefully curving arc—brought the flame directly to the tip of the second candle. He held steady while the wick ignited. Carefully he lowered the candlelighter and delivered it safely back to the usher. Only then did his craggy face broaden into a smile.

"This is the Candle of Hope!" he announced, while retrieving his cane. "Or . . . oh dear . . . maybe it's this one over here. For the life of me, I can't remember." He took his glasses back off and searched the front pews. "I don't suppose there's anything wrong with having two Candles of Hope," he said, fixing his eyes on Max. "It's good to have two," he said softly. Then Papa Jordan took his cane, planted it in front of him, and set forth on another long journey.

3
New Girl

8:48 a.m.

Ernest Graves flicked on the classroom lights, put down his Bible, and rolled up his scarf. With a nifty fold and a twist he swaddled his gloves inside his hat. Then he slid them into the sleeves of his jacket and hung it up.

Unzipping the leather cover of his Bible, he opened it to John 3:16, for good luck. Next, he straightened all the chairs. He stopped at the pencil sharpener to check the tips of his *Pray at All Times* pencils. At the Attendance Chart, he put an X next to his name. He was replacing the broken chalk with a fresh piece when the twins rushed in.

"Oh good, she's not here yet," said Rose.

"Miss Gloria is never early," Ernest reminded her.

"Not Miss Gloria," said Lily. "Amber."

The girls scurried to the coatrack. Ernest pushed the button on his wristwatch to activate its stopwatch. He watched the seconds go by. Their Sunday coat routine clocked in at exactly two minutes and 48 seconds, a ten-second gain over last week.

9:03 a.m.

Lily broke the fresh piece of chalk in two. Using the side of one piece and the tip of the other, she wrote, "Welcome, Amber," in swirling, old-fashioned letters. Frank came in with Max and tossed his jacket over a chair. The door closed behind them. Max looked up, let his jacket drop, and asked, "Who's Amber?"

22

Before he got an answer, something blue flew through the air and hit the Attendance Chart. "Goal!" shouted Rose.

"My jacket!" shouted Max.

"Next time try the coatrack," said Lily, and tossed it back to him. She and Rose began taking faded pilgrims and fall leaves down from the bulletin board.

"Will one of you please tell us what is going on?" asked Frank.

They were tidying up for Amber Everly's visit. Her family had just moved to Hillsborough from Peacham. The Noels had brought them a casserole, and after meeting Amber, the twins had invited her to Sunday School.

"Just what we need," groaned Max, "another girl."

Ernest frowned. It was hard enough just trying to fit in with Frank, Max, Rose, and Lily. The thought of a new classmate–girl or boy–made his palms sweat. Dear God, if it is thy will, take thou this cup from me, he prayed.

"How late is Miss Gloria now?" moaned Frank.

"Seventeen minutes," said Ernest, "but consider it a blessing. Her tardiness gives us a reason to practice the patience of our biblical forebears."

Max snorted. Ernest lifted his feet off the floor and shook them.

"What are you doing?" asked Frank.

"Shaking the dust off my feet. Matthew 10:14."

"What dust?" Frank dove under the table.

"I'm sorry to keep you all waiting," said Miss Gloria. "Today's lesson is on . . . Ooh!" she exclaimed. "What's that?"

"Just me," said Frank, reappearing from below. "I'm sorry, Miss Gloria. I was checking for dust. Ernest here says there's . . ."

"Never mind about the dust," interjected Ernest. "May we begin our lesson?"

23

"Not without Amber!" cried Lily and Rose. They told Miss Gloria about the new girl. "She's never been to a church before," said Lily, "but she said she'd meet us here."

It was now 9:23. Had Amber forgotten? Had she overslept? Gotten lost? Come down with the flu? The twins came up with every reason under the sun to explain her absence. Every reason except one, thought Ernest. Maybe she never meant to come in the first place.

"Rose, you go outside and check the front steps," said Miss Gloria. "Lily, you tell Mrs. Button to look for her. Then try the church office." She faced the boys. "Today's lesson is on . . ."

"Wait!" interrupted Frank. "We need another chair."

"And an extra snack," said Max, pointing to the tray of crackers and punch cups.

"And parchment for our scrolls! Dear me . . . I'll check the Craft Room," and Miss Gloria hurried out after the two boys.

9:31 a.m.

Ernest straightened the chairs again. He was putting Xs next to everyone's name on the Attendance Chart when the door opened. In came Claire Fixler, the Associate Pastor, and behind her stood a curious-looking child wearing overalls, beads, and a kerchief. Ernest stared. "Where are the others?" Pastor Claire asked.

"The others? Oh, they're out on reconnaissance for a new girl. Someone who's never been to a church in all her life. But I doubt she'll show up. She doesn't sound very . . ."

"Amber," said Pastor Claire to the child in overalls, "meet Ernest Graves. Ernest, meet Amber Everly, a friend of the Noels. Please keep her company until your classmates return."

Pastor Claire left and Ernest panicked. Instead of saying something normal, like hello, he blurted out, "I was glad when they said unto me let us go into the house of the LORD.'"

"Cool," replied Amber. "Is that a poem?"

"No. It's a psalm. P-S-A-L-M."

Amber smiled, but Ernest was too nervous to smile back. He forced himself to squint, which turned the corners of his mouth up into the shape of a smile, and that was the best he could do. He and Amber stood this way until Miss Gloria returned with Frank and Max. When the twins rushed in, squealing and flinging their arms around Amber as if she'd been gone for years, Ernest drew back to a far corner of the table.

"Today's lesson was going to be on waiting for the Messiah," Miss Gloria said.

"But we got all waiting and no Messiah," Frank grumbled.

"God's people waited hundreds of years for the Messiah. Like them, we wait with hope for the Messiah to return at the End of Time. And speaking of time . . ."

The children joined hands for the closing prayer. "Teach us, dear God, the lessons of waiting. Bless us with hope in every situation. In Christ's name we pray. Amen."

9:50 a.m.

4

Mr. Everly's Gift

Amber sat on the living room floor remembering the morning's events. The worship bulletin she'd saved as a souvenir lay open in front of her. Moving boxes labeled **LVG RM** loomed large along one wall. The shelves on the opposite wall were filled with books, and the rest of the room was bare.

After Sunday School, the twins had brought Amber to the sanctuary for worship, and now, a few hours later, everything was a glorious jumble in her mind: the robes and candles, the standing and sitting, the singing, the silence, the rumbling low notes of the organ, the swelling of prayers, and the steady thrumming of Pastor Theo's voice.

Call to Worship. Amber read the opening line several times before she thought of consulting the dictionary.

Worship: reverence paid to God or a sacred personage.

Reverence: an attitude of deep awe.

Awe: a feeling of overwhelming reverence . . .

So much for the dictionary. She revisited the bulletin. Words such as *Gloria Patri, Psalter,* and *Benediction* stared up at her, revealing nothing. She crumpled up the bulletin, and closed the dictionary with a terrific flap. Just then Mr. Everly walked in with another stack of boxes for the living room.

"More books?" Amber asked.

"You seem frustrated," her father replied.

"I'll never understand these church words."

"Were you expecting to learn them all this afternoon?"

"No, but one or two would have been nice. The dictionary was no help," she said, lifting it back onto the shelf. "Did you know there's a book in the church that's even bigger than a dictionary?"

"Yes. The Bible."

"Its pages are golden, but only on the edges, I think."

A knock on the door interrupted their conversation. "It's Rose and Lily," called Mrs. Everly. They had come to invite Amber to the Christmas Eve service.

"It's at nighttime," Rose explained, "and we use candles."

"Real candles," said Lily. "We light them at the end and sing a carol about Jesus."

"Can I go, Mom?" asked Amber. Mrs. Everly called Mrs. Noel to check on the details, and then the girls made a plan.

❄ ❄ ❄ ❄ ❄

Amber stayed near her mother for most of the day on Christmas Eve. They unpacked a few boxes and finished their Christmas cards. Mrs. Everly wrote the addresses, and Amber sealed and stamped the envelopes. Jake Everly's Can't Fail Holiday Stew simmered on the stove all afternoon. Amber wrote a letter to Carly, her best friend from Peacham, and started another one to her cousins.

Night fell sooner than Amber expected. The family gathered in the dining room. Her mother lit the dinner candles and sat down at the table across from Amber. Her father brought in a tureen full of stew and delivered it with a bow. Amber giggled. They raised their cider glasses.

"To our new home," said her father.

"To our new friends," said her mother.

"To . . . everybody here," said Amber, which for some reason made her think about Carly. They clinked, sipped, and dug into their stew. Amber missed the sweetly spiced and generously buttered hunks of gingerbread that her mother usually served up warm with the stew. The gingerbread pans weren't in any of the boxes they had opened thus far. There were no decorations, either, so when Amber finished eating, she sat and watched the candles burn. The candles reminded her of the Christmas Eve service, and that reminded her of a question.

"What's so important about Jesus?" she asked.

"I expect you'll be hearing about that tonight," said her father.

"Why don't you and Mom come with us?"

"We have things to do here."

Before Amber could ask, What things? she heard the twins knocking. It was time to go. She opened the door for Rose and Lily and then ran for her coat. When she got back, her father held out a small, flat, rectangular package.

"For me?" Amber wasn't expecting any gifts until tomorrow.

"Go ahead; open it." Her father watched her keenly. His gift to Amber was a book with pages edged in gold.

"Like the Bible," said Amber. "But there's no title. And the pages . . . they're blank?"

"It's a book for you to fill with your own words," he said. "Take it with you tonight and whenever you go to church. Write down your questions and ideas. Write down anything you want to remember, or discuss with us, or think about on your own." He put a new pencil with a good soft eraser in her coat pocket.

Amber's mother fastened her top button, knotted her scarf, and kissed her good-bye. "Have a wonderful time at the service," she said, waving them off.

"Why do they call it service?" Amber asked, after they'd walked a ways. The twins didn't know.

"Put that down in your book," said Lily. Amber balanced her new notebook on one knee and wrote her first entry by the light of a street lamp: "Service–why?"

Arm in arm with her new friends, Amber walked on into the night. She was thinking about books with golden pages, hot-buttered gingerbread, and Jesus.

5
The Beautiful Tangle

In a shallow basket, tiny metal bells strung on sleek, red ribbons glinted in the soft light of Claire Fixler's reading lamp. Claire and Theo would give them to the children during the service tonight, so she had placed them side-by-side in long, neat rows, so they wouldn't tangle. It was Christmas Eve, and she wanted everything to be perfect.

When it was time for the service to begin, Claire went to join Theo. Knocking, she nudged open his study door. Wads of paper spilled out of the wastebasket and under the desk, where Theo sat, staring. He looked like a schoolchild stuck on the first sentence of a book report, Claire thought. "Are you ready?" she asked.

Theo startled. "Am I ready? Certainly! Yes, of course I am, in a manner of speaking. At least, I hope so . . ." He stood up and started for the door, empty-handed.

"Your sermon!" exclaimed Claire. She reached for the papers he'd left behind on his desk. What? They were blank! Theo just shrugged his shoulders, but Claire panicked. She bent down and smoothed out some of the crumpled pieces from the floor. At least they had some writing on them! "You'd better use these," she advised, but Theo waved them away. "Something will come to me," he said, distractedly.

When they reached the narthex, Claire handed the basket of bells to Hal Louis, who was one of the ushers.

30

Then she and Theo fell in line behind the choir. "O come, all ye faithful, joyful and triumphant . . ." They entered the sanctuary, singing.

Claire couldn't decide whether she felt worried or angry. The Reverend Theophilus Hartiswell, Theo, had begun his ministry at The Church of the Least of These when Claire was about the age of the Noel twins. She had joined him as the Associate Pastor just over a year ago. "Wise" and "dependable" were the words she would have used to describe Theo, that is, until tonight.

❄✳❄✳❄

"The shepherds returned, glorifying and praising God for all they had heard and seen." Claire finished the last of the readings and invited the children forward. As they were scrambling down from laps and sliding past bony knees, she nodded to Hal. He strode forward with the basket of necklaces, turning this way and that, and wishing a "Merry Christmas!" to all and sundry on both sides of the aisle. As he drew near the chancel, he failed to notice Papa Jordan's cane poking out a few inches from the front pew. Catching his toe on the tip of it, Hal tripped and fell. Bells and ribbons went flying. Plonk-a-ching-ching!

"Oh dear," he said, pulling himself up to his knees. "Let's get these picked up, shall we?" He swept his large hands across the carpet and gathered them all back up. "All's well that ends well," he said, delivering them to Claire. "Praise the Lord!" Claire forced herself to smile as she sat down with Theo and the children on the chancel steps.

"These are the bells of Christmas," said Theo, giving the basket a tap.

"The joyful bells of Christmas," Claire added, brightly. "Jesus' birthday brings joy to the world, and we've got a shiny bell for each one of you! When you get back to your seats, Pastor Theo will preach the Christmas Eve sermon, and I want you to listen verrrrrrrrrrry carefully. When you hear the words 'Joy to the World!' ring your bells, all of you." That was the plan, anyway. Claire wondered if it would work.

She and Theo each took a handful of necklaces from the basket, but a ribbon in Theo's handful was looped around one of Claire's bells. They let go and tried again, but more necklaces were intertwined than before. Claire emptied the basket into her lap.

Plonk-a-ching-ching! Even so, she was unable to pick up a single bell without the whole jangling mass rising with it. She started untangling the necklaces one by one. Her fingers worked quickly, but not quickly enough.

"I can help," offered one of the children.

"So can I."

"Me too!"

"Try not to pull," whispered Claire, but pull they did. The vexing tangle soon became a hopeless knot. Oh dear God, now what? She looked over at Theo. He was rubbing his chin, lost in thought. But here came Hal, thank heavens, with a pair of scissors. "Everybody, let go!" Claire said, as she took the scissors from him. "Scoot back everybody, a little farther, that's better, while I cut these apart. It's not what I planned, but it's the best I can do."

She brought the scissors to the knotted ribbons and was about to snip, when she felt a tug on the sleeve of her robe. It was Lily Noel. "Don't cut them, Pastor Claire!" Lily whispered. "Look—they're beautiful the way they are!" Claire stopped short. Lily traced the curl of a ribbon with her forefinger, then reached her hand into the cluster of bells and shook them lightly. Ching-a-ring, ching-a-ring!

Claire realized that Lily was right: the bells were more beautiful together than they would be cut apart. She handed the scissors safely back to Hal, and while she sat puzzling over this, Theo jumped to his feet. With a wave of his arm he sent the startled children back to the pews, seized the bells from Claire, and stepped up to the pulpit. "Life is full of twists and turns," he declared, holding up the necklaces. "One day brings a delightful surprise. Another, a bitter disappointment."

He turned the knot over in his hands and studied it from different angles before going on. "Things don't always happen according to plan," he said, gently. "Sometimes our good ideas turn out poorly. Sometimes our efforts to help only make things worse. But none of this matters, not on Christmas Eve nor on any other day of the year. God puts all our efforts to good use. God's plan is the one that matters."

While marveling at Theo's sudden transformation, Claire was surprised to hear him call her name. He was beckoning her to join him at the pulpit! "In God's plan, we don't go through the twists and turns of life alone," Theo said, making room for Claire to stand next to him. "Our efforts combine." Theo traced the line of a single ribbon as it intersected others. "Our lives intertwine. We are bound together in the beautiful tangle of everyday living, and Jesus Christ–who was born this night–is everywhere among us. Nothing in heaven or on earth can cut us off from him, or from each other. He is Emmanuel, which means God-with-us!"

Theo pressed the clump of necklaces into Claire's hands. "Joy to the World!" he cried. Claire shook the tangled bells: ching-a-ring, ching-a-ring! "Joy to the World!!" he cried again, this time bidding the congregation to say it with him. Ching-a-ring, ching-a-ring, ching-a-ring! "Joy to the World!!!" they cried, once more.

Claire went on ringing and ringing, even after the tears came. Tears of joy. They streamed down her face. Theo's, too. And somewhere nearby–Claire imagined–they were streaming down the face of God, as well.

Pink Jesus

Max kicked a hockey puck across the Sunday School room floor to Ernest. "I wanted to bring my new hockey stick too, but my dad wouldn't let me. What did you get for Christmas?" he asked.

"Um, just some books and stuff," said Ernest, kicking the puck sideways to Frank. Rose hovered nearby, her eyes on the puck, but Lily watched disinterestedly. When Amber opened her gold-edged notebook and asked her for an interview, Lily readily agreed. They moved to the far end of the table and sat down, heads close together.

"Full name?" asked Amber.

"Lily Jeannette Noel."

"Place of birth?"

"Hillsborough."

"Reason for coming here today?"

"I always come."

"Reason for always coming?"

"I always come because . . ." A pink crayon caught Lily's eye. She picked it up and glanced around for a piece of scrap paper. Oblivious to the noise from the other end of the room, and forgetting all about Amber's questions, Lily started to sketch. She drew a pink cow and a pink donkey. She drew pink sheep and shepherds, pink camels, and a few pink chickens. In the center, a pink Mary and Joseph knelt before a pink baby Jesus.

"You're an artist!" exclaimed Amber, but Lily didn't look up until she'd added a host of pink angels gliding through a sky studded with bright pink stars. Finally she held her drawing out at arm's length and smiled.

"Oh, that baby is cute enough to be a girl," she said, and quickly added a pink hair bow to the head of baby Jesus. It was the kind of bow that mothers paste on the heads of their bald girl babies. Then she put down her crayon. "Tah-dah!"

Frank called for a time-out to look at Lily's drawing. Soon everyone had gathered around her. "Too bad they're all pink," said Max.

"Hey, that's not right. She's got a girl baby in there!" Ernest was beside himself. "You've got to change that, right now," he told Lily.

"Calm down," Rose defended her sister. "It's just a doodle."

"No. It's a sacrilege. 'For God so loved the world that he gave his only Son . . .'" But before Ernest could finish, Lily converted the hair bow into a pair of animal ears jutting out from behind Jesus' head.

The door opened. "Good morning!" Miss Gloria emptied her tote bag onto the table. "I'm sorry to keep you waiting. Today is Epiphany Sunday. E-P-I-P-H-A-N-Y." She wrote the word on the chalkboard and Amber copied it into her notebook. "Do you remember the story we heard on Christmas Eve–before the bells got tangled?

"Wise men from a faraway country followed a bright star in search of Jesus. They finally found him on the day we now call Epiphany. Jesus looked like any other baby born into a poor family, but the wise men saw him differently. Something clicked," Miss Gloria snapped her fingers. "They knelt before him and presented him with gifts that only a king would be given: gold, frankincense, and myrrh. Questions, anyone?"

"Lily drew a picture of that," said Max. "It could've been a masterpiece, but it's pink." Amber asked how to spell "myrrh" and "frankincense" so she could write them in her notebook correctly. Then Rose had a question.

"If Jesus had been a girl, what would God have named her?"

Lily giggled, Ernest scowled, but Miss Gloria grew thoughtful. "The name Jesus means, God saves. It comes from the Hebrew name Joshua, but that's also a boy's name, isn't it? Hmmm . . . Why do you ask?"

"Lily drew a little bow on Jesus' head, just for fun, but when Ernest complained she changed it to animal ears. Right here," Rose showed Miss Gloria the exact spot on the drawing. "That got me thinking, why was Jesus a boy? God could have made him a girl if God wanted to, right?"

"Why, yes, I suppose so."

"The Bible doesn't have enough girls in it."

"True," said Miss Gloria.

"The Bible is perfect the way it is," huffed Ernest.

"That's true too," said Miss Gloria. "We can't change the Bible," she went on, "nor can we change the way people lived in Bible times. Girls and women weren't free to be leaders back then, but thankfully," she snapped her fingers again, "we are now. If God had made Jesus a girl, what do you think would be a good name for her?"

"Sunny," said Rose, "because Jesus is the light of the world."

Miss Gloria wrote S-U-N-N-Y on the chalkboard just under E-P-I-P-H-A-N-Y.

"How about Joy?" suggested Amber. "Her name could be Joy because of what Pastor Theo said about the bells." The room suddenly became quiet.

Finally Frank spoke up. "That's not a bad idea, Amber. I think Joy would've been a good name if Jesus was a girl . . ."

"BUT HE WASN'T!" roared Ernest.

"How about two names," suggested Rose, "Sunny and Joy? 'Sunny Joy,' just like Jesus and Christ make 'Jesus Christ.'"

Time was up. "Who will lead our closing prayer?" asked Miss Gloria.

"You do it," Frank told Lily. "Your drawing got us into this argument." He snatched it away from her, but then stopped short. "You ruined it!"

The children crowded around to see what he meant. While everyone else was talking, Lily had colored over her drawing with a black crayon.

"What'd you go and do that for?" asked Max.

"Well, for Epiphany," Lily explained. "You know, with the wise men."

"Pardon me, but I can't quite make out the wise men," said Frank, squinting and turning the paper upside down.

"You're not supposed to," said Lily. "You're supposed to see what they saw."

Lily's picture was now all black except for a pink and white circle—about the size of a hockey puck—where the original drawing showed through. In the circle was the face of baby Jesus. A pair of pink animal ears poked up jauntily from the background. Strands of pink hay streamed outward like rays of sunshine. Baby Jesus smiled, from ear to ear.

7
Doves by the Thousands

Every Sunday, Pearl Button, the Superintendent of the Sunday School, began her rounds by checking for messages. Today, a note from Theo read, "Pearl: Annual meeting after worship today. Child care needed." Pearl thought for a moment. The Noel girls were reliable. She would ask them.

On her way to the classroom, Pearl recognized Ernest Graves walking a few paces ahead of her. A child she didn't recognize trotted alongside, asking him questions.

"Full name?"

"Ernest Wesley Graves."

"Reason for coming?"

"To receive edification for the sanctification of my soul."

Pearl changed her plan. "Good morning!" she trilled. The children turned around to look at her. "Ernest, we need volunteers to watch the preschoolers during the annual meeting. You'll help, won't you?"

"Yes ma'am," said Ernest.

"And your friend?"

"My what?"

"Sure, I'll help," said the child.

"Wonderful," said Pearl. "Ernest, will you introduce your friend?"

"My what?"

"I'm Amber Everly. I'm new."

"Hello Amber, I'm Mrs. Button."

"How are you at spelling?" asked Amber. "Ernie, what did you say was your reason for coming here?"

"Ernest, not Ernie."

Pearl spelled out "edification" and "sanctification" for Amber, who printed the words in the handsome notebook she was carrying. "Mrs. Scuttle will be expecting you right after worship," said Pearl, "so don't dawdle."

Pearl nudged open the door to Merrilee Scuttle's classroom. Around a kiddie pool filled with water sat a group of wide-eyed children. Merrilee had just begun telling the Bible story.

"When Jesus grew to be a man, he was baptized in a river." She plunged both hands into the pool. Squealing with glee, the children drew up their own handfuls of water and let it spill back out through their fingers. Triggle-triggle. They shook their hands dry and spread out around the room. "Arms up, everybody. While Jesus was being baptized, the Holy Spirit came down from heaven like a dove. Coo, coo." Merrilee flapped her arms. The children flapped their arms, too, and fluttered about the room, calling, "coo, coo." Merrilee flapped her way over to Pearl, who whispered for her to expect Ernest and Amber after worship. Merrilee nodded and circled back to the children. Slowing to a stop, she folded her imaginary wings and came to rest in a kneeling position. The children folded their wings too, and perched on the rug.

"Then the voice of God said . . ." Merrilee held her finger to her lips. So did the children. "'This is my own dear Son,'" she whispered. "'Listen to him.'" They leaned forward and listened in the stillness.

✿ ✾ ✽ ✾ ✿

The annual meeting started with committee reports. Pearl didn't care for committee reports. Her mind wandered, and soon she slipped out to the Ladies' Room. There, she heard the short, quick breaths of a child trying to cry without making a sound. Pearl knocked on the door of the stall. "I'm Mrs. Button," she said. "Who are you? You sound terribly sad."

"I'm . . . I'm . . . Amber, the new girl."

"Amber! Whatever is the matter? Will you tell me? I can listen from here, or maybe you'll open the door? There's a dear girl. No one should have to cry alone. I've got a handkerchief–much softer on the nose than toilet tissue."

Amber splashed water on her face and asked to see Rose or Lily. Pearl took her to Fellowship Hall. The twins spotted their friend right away and scurried over. Frank and Max followed more slowly, but Ernest hung back.

"Amber!" cried Lily.

"What's wrong?" asked Rose.

"I was helping Ernest in the preschool room. We made a circle to play 'duck-duck-goose,' but Ernest taught the children to say, 'baptized-baptized-heathen.' I'm not baptized, Mrs. Button, and my parents don't even go to church. Am I . . . a heathen?"

Ernest drew near. "It was not my intention to throw you into agony over the condition of your mortal soul," he told Amber. "'We are all born in the pollution of sin and are the children of wrath,' says the Second Helvetic Confession, 'but God, who is rich in mercy, freely cleanses us from our sins by the blood of his Son.'"

Frank raised his hand like a traffic cop. "Whoa!" he spoke sharply to Ernest. "Don't say another word." He turned to Amber. "Trust me, he's the only one around here who talks like that."

"We must all work out our own salvation with fear and trembling," Ernest added. "Philippians 2:12."

Frank grabbed Ernest by the knot of his tie. Pearl held her breath. "You and your Second Palpatetic Confessions," growled Frank, "and your fear and trembling, and your pollution and wrath. How come you're always quoting something creepy?" He let go of Ernest and backed off, although he was clearly still angry. Pearl exhaled. Ernest lifted one foot off the ground and shook it. He did the same with the other, and turned to leave.

"Well," said Amber.

"Well what, dearie?" asked Pearl.

"You never answered my question."

Pearl took Amber aside. She told her the story Merrilee had acted out with the pre-schoolers. When she got to the part with all the doves fluttering and cooing around the room, Amber finally smiled.

"I can't imagine God keeping the Holy Spirit cooped up inside one little dove," Pearl told Amber. "The way I see it, God flings open the heavens every day, sending down doves by the thousands."

8
Drenched

Constance Grumble arrived early the following Sunday and went directly to the church kitchen. She was in charge of today's Coffee Hour, but Gloria Kelsey had called earlier to say that the children in her Sunday School class wanted to help. What they really wanted, she'd discovered, was to turn the Coffee Hour into a "snowflake theme party" for Frank Treadwell's baby sister, Maeve, who was to be baptized during the service. Constance had mixed feelings. Coffee Hour should be a dignified gathering, not a children's carnival. Even so, she was intrigued by the snowflake theme and had brought a little something of her own to add to the decorations.

As Constance filled the large coffeemaker with water and measured out the coffee, the children trickled in. She set out the good tablecloths and then began to unwrap the small, round parcel she'd brought with her. The children came over to watch. "When I heard about your snowflake theme, I decided to bring my doilies," she said, without looking up. "They're the handiwork of three generations of women in my family. They'll add a nice touch to the tables, if you'd like to use them."

"Heirlooms?" whispered Amber.

"Each one is different," observed Lily.

"Like snowflakes," said Max.

"Like babies," said Rose.

"Are they machine washable?" asked Ernest.

The children soon drifted away, all except for Amber. She lingered over each doily, pointing out their similarities and differences and asking question after question, until Constance herself saw details she'd never noticed before.

For her baptism, Maeve wore a gown whose layered petticoats rippled merrily whenever she kicked her tiny feet. Looking handsome in a jacket and tie, Frank carefully poured the water from the crystal pitcher into the baptismal font. But Constance couldn't keep her mind on the baptism. She was thinking about Amber.

Up until now she'd had an unfavorable view of the girl, no doubt because of the way she dressed. For Constance, proper Sunday clothing was a matter of respect, but Amber hadn't shown her an ounce of disrespect the whole time they'd spent together examining the doilies. As a matter of fact, thought Constance, the girl was delightful.

She turned to wondering about Amber's mother and father. What must they be like, sending their child off to church in overalls and a T-shirt? Maybe they didn't know any better. Maybe they couldn't afford better. Slowly, it dawned on Constance that she had never seen Amber with either a mother or a father. As far as she could recall, the girl had simply appeared one Sunday with no introduction and no explanations. Good heavens! Was that little slip of a thing somebody's foster child?

Theo nestled Maeve in the crook of one arm. "In baptism God adopts us into the household of faith," he said. "By water and the Holy Spirit, God joins us to Christ and to the church, which is his body." Then Theo drew up the first of three handfuls of water. "Maeve Irene, I baptize you in the name of the Father," triggle-triggle, "and of the Son," triggle-triggle, "and of the Holy Spirit," triggle-triggle.

Theo always overdid it with the water, Constance thought. All that sloshing spoiled the charm.

❄❄❄❄❄

During the Coffee Hour after worship, Constance kept watch over the punch bowl. That way she could also keep an eye on Amber, who along with Max was one of the servers. "Hold the ladle over the bowl and fill each cup only half full. Red punch stains terribly. Mind the doilies and especially the baby's gown."

Snowflake-themed treats provided by the children were a big hit. There was something for everyone's taste: Sno Caps, frosted flakes, macaroon snowmen, pineapple snow pudding, and even sugar-cube igloos for the preschoolers. Gloria kept Ernest and

the twins busy refilling punch cups and fetching treats, napkins, and coffee. Constance received many compliments on the crocheted doilies.

Hal's voice boomed out over the crowd. "This is a one-of-a-kind celebration for a one-of-a-kind baby!" He took Maeve in his arms and spun her round and round.

"May I cut in?" asked Earl Button, and soon Maeve was being waltzed around the room and passed from one set of arms to another. Finally Maeve announced with a terrific "Waaaaah" that she'd had enough. Mrs. Treadwell threaded toward her.

"Maeve, honey, here I am," she called. "You're OK, sweetie pie. Mommy's coming." But Maeve wailed louder than ever, wriggling and twisting in the direction of the voice she loved. As mother and baby stretched out their arms, the spectators backed away.

"Watch out!" yelled Amber, but it was too late. The spectators backed right into the serving table. Amber grasped the punch bowl with both hands even as a wave of red sploshed over the rim and all down the front of her.

"Good heavens!" exclaimed Constance. She led Amber into the kitchen and pressed a damp cloth to the bright red splotches on her overalls. Over and over, she praised Amber for her quick thinking, which had saved the church's good punch bowl from shattering. After Constance rinsed and wrung out the cloth, Amber gasped. "Your heirloom, Mrs. Grumble, it's ruined!"

Sure enough, in her haste Constance had used one of her antique doilies to work on the spill, and it was now ruby red. At any other time Constance would have considered this a catastrophe, but right now she was concerned about Amber. "Never mind the doily," she said, tossing it aside and drying her hands. "It might end up slightly pink after it's washed, but that won't be the end of the world." Constance patted her on the head. "It's only a doily, after all, and it was there when we needed it–a small sacrifice, for a good cause."

9
Sticks and Stones

Hal Louis opened the bedroom window and stuck his head out, nose up. The sky's celestial blue was more than a color—it was a taste, a smell, a sensation of being drawn heavenward. "Good morning, God!" he cried. Then he closed his eyes and held very still. Pssssssst, his whiskers rippled. "Light winds from the north-northwest. Temperature"—he rubbed his nose—"just below freezing." Everything pointed to near perfect conditions for today's skating party.

Hal put on his glasses and pulled the window shut. He could see faraway things without them, but up close was one big blur. He depended on his glasses almost as much as he depended on God.

Soon Hal zipped up his duffel bag of gear, slung his skates over his shoulder, and headed down the road to Faeron's Pond. He stopped first at the General Store, which was on the way.

"Morning, Hal," said Charles Chipman, the storekeeper. "Have you got everything you need for the party?" He took an ACE bandage down from the shelf and put it on the counter. Charles was good at guessing what his customers wanted, but this time he was wrong.

"I'm putting my trust in the Lord," said Hal, waving away the bandage. "If God wants us to have this party, then God won't let anything ruin it. Not even a sprained ankle." Charles changed the subject to cocoa, and said he'd have it ready for the kids by noon.

When Hal bought a roll of breath mints Charles asked, "Somebody special?" Hal blushed and stuffed the mints into his pocket. Gloria Kelsey was coming to help him with the party and he wanted to ask her for a date, if he could find the courage. Hal turned to leave. "Hold on," said Charles, and tossed him the ACE bandage. "Take it just in case," he said. "It's on the house."

The footpath to Faeron's Pond began behind the General Store. In the meadow beyond, clusters of Queen Anne's lace bowed in the breeze. The slender leaves of cattails quivered like harp strings thrumming a thousand glissandos. A mockingbird rehearsed its repertoire of piccolo trills, oboe drones, and the whooo-meee? of a slide whistle. Hal moved silently among them.

❋❋❋❋❋

By mid-morning the party was in full swing. Hal and Gloria sat and talked together as they watched the skaters. Little tykes scissor-stepped on the ice, crying, "Look at me. I'm skating!" Teenagers in pairs practiced hockey stops and forward crossovers. Alone in a corner of the pond, Rose Noel leaped into the air, turned, and landed on one foot–a magnificent waltz jump. "To think this party almost didn't happen!" Gloria said, shaking her head in wonder.

"It really is a miracle," murmured Hal, and his thoughts turned to the events of the past week.

❋❋❋❋❋

After Maeve's "snowflake" baptism, the teenagers in the Youth Group had asked to throw a party of their own—an outdoor skating party for all the children. But when the invitations went out, Allegra Tremblay and Georgie Handelbach burst into tears—they wanted to go but they didn't own skates. Neither did half the children in the Sunday School. The Blythe family children owned one pair between the five of them, and it was too small for Billy and Tillie but too large for the others.

Pastor Claire called an emergency meeting, and everyone blamed Hal. "You're the Youth Group Adviser," they said. "You should have known better." They called him "uncaring" and "irresponsible." One parent threatened a boycott. Another demanded his resignation. Hal's spirits sank lower and lower, when suddenly Constance Grumble stood up and signaled for quiet.

"This town is full of skates," she snapped. "I have two pairs hanging in my attic. Nothing fancy, but a skate's a skate. If you'll stop bickering and work together, every child without skates will have a pair in time for the party. We'll need names and shoe sizes for starters." She held up a clipboard. "Meeting adjourned."

Wonder of wonders, the skates poured in. Handyman Forest McNutt sharpened the blades in his workshop. Charles Chipman replaced broken laces with new ones from the General Store. The teenagers polished the boots, and Pastor Theo buffed them until they shone. "Loaves and fishes," he said, as he inspected each boot. "Loaves and fishes."

❄❄❄❄❄

Hal was thinking about miracles when Gloria tugged his sleeve. Maybe he should ask her for a date right now, right this instant, he thought. But Gloria had jumped up and was pulling him toward the ice. Hal followed her and saw Lizbeth Scuttle sitting on the ice, crying. "She pitched forward as if she'd caught her skate on something," Gloria told him as they helped Lizbeth over to the bench. When Hal went back to check the ice where Lizbeth and her friends had been skating, he found sticks and branches strewn about randomly. All were freshly broken.

"I cleared off every inch of this pond before the party," he told Gloria. He hoped this wasn't somebody's idea of a prank.

Suddenly there came a shout of alarm. Hal sped toward another group of children. They were huddled around Rose Noel, who lay on the ice holding her left shin, her face contorted with pain. Thweeeep! Hal blew the emergency whistle and the teenagers streamed in from all points. "Royal, you help me get Rose over to the clearing. Integrity, you check the ice. Skating's over," he told the others.

Mr. Noel arrived just as the paramedics were lifting Rose into an ambulance. Hal promised to join them at the hospital as soon as he could get away. After the ambulance drove off, Hal walked into the General Store. The children stopped talking and gathered round, their faces solemn. "Is Rose badly hurt?" asked Ernest Graves, adding that he had missed the skating because of an unexpected visit from a relative.

"She's got an ugly bump, maybe a hairline fracture," said Hal.

"How did it happen?"

"Integrity found a handful of stones near where Rose was skating. We think someone was aiming at her from behind the bushes."

"Billy Blythe," said Max. "If you want my opinion, that's who did it. He's a thug, and he can throw really well." But Billy overheard Max, and he walked straight up to him and looked him square in the eye. "Did you say thug? Only chickens talk about someone else behind their back." Billy flapped his elbows and clucked. Then all the Blythe family children threw down their borrowed skates and walked out.

Was Gloria still there? As Hal pushed his glasses up his nose to look for her, they snapped in two at the bridge. He caught one side, but the other clattered to the floor. "Oh, Lord," he said, and dropped to his knees patting blindly.

Pastor Claire suggested a sing-along. "Any requests?" she asked. There were none. "We all know 'Morning Has Broken,' don't we?" Hal's nose bumped against the missing half of his glasses. He saw a cloudy image of himself reflected in the lens. Like a tiny pond, he thought, under an immense, gray sky. Tucking both halves into his shirt pocket, he stood up, and sang out sadly into the blur.

Pilgrims' Protest

A few Sundays later, when Gloria nudged open the classroom door, the children's wrinkled foreheads and frowns told her something was up. Pastor Claire was making an announcement. Gloria stepped quietly inside. "Surely you remember the marvelous job Mr. Wigglenot's class did last year," said Claire. "Now it's your turn to shine. Any questions?"

"What's the play about?" Amber asked, turning to a fresh page in her notebook.

"Excellent!" Claire rubbed her palms together as if she was investigating a spine-tingling mystery. "Who can tell Amber what *Pilgrim's Progress* is about?" Her question met with a stiff silence, so Claire read from the script:

"The Pilgrim's Progress, written by John Bunyan in the year 1678, takes us on a perilous adventure with the hero, Christian, as he journeys from the City of Destruction to the Celestial City, by way of the Cross."

"Why do we always do the same play?" Frank asked.

"Another excellent question!" Claire read on:

"Adapted for stage, *Pilgrim's Progress* is performed by the middle elementary Sunday School class every year on Anniversary Sunday."

"Yeah, but why?" said Frank.

Gloria put her tote bag down loudly on her desk and walked over to Claire. "I'll take it from here," she whispered to her. "Class, please thank Pastor Claire for her visit."

The moment Claire left, Max raised his hand, but he didn't wait to be called on. "Miss Gloria, my dad fell asleep during the play last year even though my brother was in it." A snort from Frank set off a round of laughter so loud that it nearly drowned out the sound of someone knocking on the door. Gloria signaled for quiet.

"Why, hello, Mrs. Grumble. Do come in. What brings you to our class this morning?"

"The Clothing Exchange Box is filled to overflowing. Can you spare a volunteer?" Without waiting for an answer, Constance peered at Amber. "I need your sharp eyes," she said. "Even with my glasses I have trouble making out the tags. You do know your numbers and letters, don't you?"

"I'm reading *Jane Eyre* and doing fractions, if that's what you mean."

While Gloria walked Amber and Mrs. Grumble to the door, Frank took the script off her desk and began reading where Claire stopped. "'Old, but ever new, *Pilgrim's Progress* is edifying for all ages.'" Frank rubbed his palms together just as Claire had done.

"Edifying. Who can tell us what that means? Ernest?"

None of this was missed on Gloria. She hurried back to the table, snatched the script away from Frank, and sat him firmly back down. "Our Bible verse for today is, 'Rejoice in the Lord always; again I will say, Rejoice.' Lily, you have lovely handwriting. Will you write these magnificent words on the chalkboard for us?"

"When are the rehearsals?" interrupted Rose. She sat with one leg up, and a ball of yarn in her lap. She'd taken up knitting to pass the time until her leg healed.

Gloria found a schedule. Saturday mornings, Wednesday afternoons, and . . .

"Saturday mornings? Awwwwwww!" Rose groaned. Frank scraped his chair back from the table and folded his arms across his chest. Max stalked over to the supply cabinet, took out some paper, and started to write. Lily printed the Bible verse on the board in heavy block letters.

"Notice how the verse begins and ends with the word *rejoice*," Gloria continued. "The apostle Paul wrote this to the church in Philippi, after he'd been jailed, beaten, shipwrecked, and stoned." She tapped Rose's cast for emphasis. "Imagine if you had to suffer–really suffer–for the Lord. Do you think you could rejoice, like Paul?"

"Ask me again after the play," said Frank. Max handed what he'd written to Frank, who nodded and passed the paper around the table. After everyone read it, they all started whispering. Gloria abandoned her lesson plan and waited.

Eventually, Lily stood up. "Miss Gloria, we protest." She pulled Max up from his chair and said, "You read it." Max grew pale and his voice wavered, but he read:

We, the children of the middle elementary Sunday School class, respectfully refuse to put on Pilgrim's Progress because:

- *It is boring.*
- *It uses too many long words that no one understands.*
- *We want to play in the snow, etc., on Saturdays.*

No hard feelings, OK?

Yours truly,

Max Wynne   Frank Treadwell
Rose Noel   Lily Noel
Ernest Graves

As Max handed the paper to Gloria, Amber burst back in the room, clutching an overstuffed brown paper bag. Her eyes glinted with fury. "Mrs. Grumble lied," she said, letting the bag drop. "The clothes were already sorted. She asked what size I wore and then she chose outfits for me!! 'Here's a pretty one.' 'Isn't this darling?' When I said, 'No thank you,' she said, 'Shhhhh,' and made me take them all."

"In case anybody is wondering," Amber's eyes narrowed into fiery slits, "I have plenty of clothes. I save my best ones, meaning my favorite ones, for church. It's my way of cheering God up a little, like it says over there on the chalkboard."

"Hey, here's my old Easter dress," announced Rose, who was picking through the clothing. "Ooh, remember this one, Lily? It was Integrity Morgan's. She hated the poofy sleeves." Rose held it up against Amber. Its short black top erupted into a skirt of pale yellow sateen. "You look like Snow White. Hey, why don't we do that show instead?" Amber smiled weakly.

Gloria's head was spinning. With just five minutes of class time left, she was tempted to dismiss the children immediately, but Rose's joke gave her a better idea. She clapped her hands until the room was quiet. "A written protest is a serious matter," she said, holding up the paper the children had signed. "I promise to support you on this, but on one condition: that you put your heads together this week and come back on Sunday with an idea of what you'd like to do instead of *Pilgrim's Progress*."

"That's easy," said Rose. "I'd like to go ice-skating, if I ever get rid of this stupid cast."

"That's not what she meant," said Ernest, and everyone began talking at once.

❀❀❀❀❀

Ten days later, Gloria found herself in the church parlor attending a meeting of the Elders. Lily, Rose, Max, Amber, Frank, and Ernest were there, too. They sat together on a deacon's bench directly opposite Claire and Theo. Their legs dangled beneath them and their upper bodies arched toward one another like a row of question marks crowded together on a practice page.

After Gloria introduced the topic, Earl Button, the Clerk, read the petition and the children's names out loud. "And instead of *Pilgrim's Progress,* you propose to put on an original ice-skating show . . . about Jesus?" he asked.

Yes, they nodded.

" . . . to be held at Faeron's Pond?"

They nodded again.

"And you are in full agreement with one another on this proposal?"

"Yes, sir. We're 100 percent unanimous," declared Max.

"Is that so?" interjected Ian Rankle. "Then why do I count one, two, three, four, five, six of you here, but only five names on the petition? If you're trying to hide something . . ." He shook his finger accusingly. The children jolted upright in their seats, a series of exclamation points.

"We're not hiding anything," snapped Amber. "When Max showed me the petition I didn't know anything about *Pilgrim's Progress.* Naturally I didn't sign it. How can you be against something you don't know anything about? Later I found out that *Pilgrim's Progress* is a classic, so I checked it out of the library. You can never go wrong with the classics, you know."

The Elders shifted in their seats. "Then you're opposed to the skating show?" asked Earl.

"Oh no. I'm all for it. Did we mention we're calling it 'The Gospel on Ice'? The name alone gives me the shivers."

Several hands went up, but Theo called on Eulalia Dawn. "I'm very pleased to have you children here with us tonight," Eulalia said, smiling warmly, "but I am not in favor of your proposal. You'll learn a great deal by putting on *Pilgrim's Progress,* even if your audience doesn't. Like Amber, I see great value in the classics."

"But I'm in favor of 'The Gospel on Ice'!" cried Amber.

Theo made sure all the Elders understood Amber's position. Then he asked, "Are you ready to vote?"

"No!" Claire's voice rang out. "Theo, I mean, Mr. Moderator, may I . . ."

"Yes, Claire. Keep it short."

"It's just that . . . oh gosh, I don't want to spoil anything, but let's not forget what happened at the skating party. Rose, I'm so relieved to see your leg out of the cast, but what if that heartless, stone-throwing coward comes back and strikes again?"

Smiles faded even before Claire finished speaking. Gloria shuddered just thinking about those awful moments at the pond. And Ernest wilted, his shoulders sagging and his chin on his chest. He took a deep breath. "That won't happen," he said flatly. "And I can guarantee it, because"–he took another deep breath–"that heartless coward was me." Ernest sat up straighter and faced his friends. "I can't skate. I knew you'd make fun of me if you found out." His chest rose and fell as he fought back tears. "So I hid in the bushes. All I could think of was how to spoil the fun. At first, it was just sticks, but during the relay races I saw Rose off by herself and I . . . Oh Rose, everybody, I'm s . . . s . . . sorry."

❄ ❄ ❄ ❄ ❄

When the vote was finally taken it was a tie, three in favor, three opposed. "The Moderator's vote breaks a tie," Gloria whispered. The children shifted their somber gaze to Theo, and Gloria held her breath.

"The Clerk shall record in the minutes that on this night," said Theo, "by a vote of four to three, approval was granted for the children of the middle elementary Sunday School class to perform 'The Gospel on Ice' on Anniversary Sunday."

Bogged Down

A few Sundays later, while Amber and her classmates were waiting for Miss Gloria, Amber decided to raise the subject they'd been squabbling about: Jesus. She had a suggestion. At first nobody liked it, but as they talked, one by one her friends came around. "Is everybody OK with this plan?" Amber finally asked. No one spoke. "Then it's settled. We'll all be Jesus. Period. End of discussion." Amber opened her notebook and wrote, "Jesus: everyone." But was it really settled? Or would the arguments start back up this afternoon at rehearsal? She was worried.

Preparations for "The Gospel on Ice" had gotten off to a smooth start. The children held a planning meeting to divide out responsibilities. Amber had been astonished when Frank asked her to be the Director.

"But I'm new," was all she could say.

"Not anymore," Ernest pointed out.

The twins were positively jubilant when she agreed, and the other jobs were easily assigned. Producer: Frank; Script: Ernest; Costumes: Lily; Scenery: Max;

Props: Rose. Pastor Theo worked with Ernest on the script, which they finished in a few days. The show began with Jesus reading from the scroll of Isaiah and causing a protest in his hometown of Nazareth. It moved on to three stories about Jesus' ministry and ended with two selections from his famous Sermon on the Mount. So far, so good, Amber recalled.

The bickering had begun over the script. "Too many thees and thous and doeths and saiths," said Frank. "It's worse than *Pilgrim's Progress!*" Next they bickered about the costumes. Lily wanted them to wear long Middle Eastern robes and head coverings. "We won't be able to see." "We'll trip and fall." "We'll all break our legs," they complained. But mostly they bickered about Jesus. Everyone had strong opinions about Jesus and everyone except Ernest wanted to be Jesus.

"He should skate smoothly, almost like he's floating," Lily had said, during yesterday's rehearsal, when they were working on Scene 1.

"That's completely wrong," said Frank. "Jesus was a real person and he should skate like one. Real people don't float."

"He was the Son of God," argued Max. "He should skate with power. When the townspeople charge toward him, he should rush the line like a quarterback." Max sped across the ice, ducked his head, and burst through an imaginary defensive line.

Rose argued that "The Gospel on Ice" should be like an outdoor ballet with Jesus as the lead dancer. "Whoever skates the best should be Jesus. I guess that's me."

"Right," said Max. "And we'll all wear tutus."

"There are no ballerinas in my script!" said Ernest. "There are no ballerinas in the Bible!! You got that, Rose?"

Amber didn't think they would ever stop arguing if she didn't do something, but what? "I should probably just pick a Jesus and get on with it," she said to her parents that night at dinner, "but how can I? Compared with them, I don't know anything about the real Jesus. Plus they're getting on my nerves."

"How about taking turns?" her father asked. Amber frowned. "If you take turns, everyone can portray Jesus from their own point of view," said Mr. Everly. "That's what preachers do."

Amber avoided her friends by going straight to the sanctuary after Sunday School and sitting alone during worship. She couldn't help yawning. Nothing interested her today. One of the hymns had a catchy tune, but Mrs. Handelbach played it too slowly on the organ. It'd be so much livelier with an accordion, Amber thought. She stopped singing to jot that down, and joined in again for the final chorus:

> In-a my heart, (in-a my heart), in-a my heart, (in-a my heart),
> Lord, I want to be like Jesus in-a my heart.

And she had another problem: the back of her neck itched. She was wearing a brand-new white blouse and she had forgotten to cut out the tags. She'd bought it after her humiliating ordeal with Mrs. Grumble and the Clothing Exchange Box. Its high collar and eggshell-thin buttons down the back had made her feel noble, like a pioneer woman, when she first tried it on. Not anymore, she said to herself.

Amber ran straight home after worship. Torpedoing into her room, she wrenched off the blouse and slithered into a cotton T-shirt. She closed the door and played a few rounds of darts with herself. Next she emptied out the pockets of all of her overalls. She tackled her sock drawer after that, and found matches for six strays. Now what?

She guessed it was time for rehearsal, but she didn't want to go. The slanting afternoon light beckoned her instead to the window seat where she kept her books. Amber pulled up an afghan and turned to chapter 6 of *Jane Eyre*. She read a paragraph, but the words didn't register. She read it three more times, and then she gave up. She needed a book that would pull her right into the story. Maybe a Nancy Drew? She chose *The Secret of the Old Clock,* but partway through the first chapter she remembered the secret and tossed the book to the floor.

Next on her stack was the library copy of *Pilgrim's Progress.* She'd left off reading just as the main character, Christian, and his traveling companion, Pliable, had fallen into a bog . . .

". . . and the name of the bog was the Slough of Despond."

She read on. After a desperate struggle, Pliable freed himself and turned back, leaving Christian alone in the mire. Deeper and deeper he sank, until Help appeared. Help pitied Christian and pulled him out. Christian journeyed onward.

Amber stopped reading and gazed out the window. What does a slough look like? she wondered. The moisture from her own breath blurred her view.

In her mind's eye she pictured a stand of cattails, marsh water the color of new pennies, snares of blackberry brambles, a fallen tree grown spongy from blue lichen, creeping moss, sprawling shelf mushrooms, and a feudal underworld of grubs, spiders, and their webs. But this couldn't be right. In order to fool somebody, an actual slough would have to seem unremarkable: a mere opening in the brush, an innocent little clearing. She thought of the clearing at the end of the footpath to Faeron's Pond, and she thought of her friends.

Suddenly one of her legs cramped. The window seat felt like a trap. She had to get out, right this second! Shaking off the afghan, she uncrossed her legs, jumped down, and hurried to the door. If she ran all the way to the pond, maybe her friends would still be there. She wanted to tell them about the Slough of Despond, and about Help coming to Christian, but mostly she wanted to tell them she wasn't mad anymore.

12
Guesswork

Frank spotted Amber running toward the pond along the footpath and skated over to meet her, with Max, Rose, and Lily following. "Wait'll you see what we came up with for Scene 1!" cried Max. "Rose thought up the perfect moves for Jesus, and I mean *perfect.*"

Rose bowed modestly, but Amber looked around. "Where's Ernest?" she asked, out of breath, but Max ignored her question.

"You should've been here," he said. "It was brilliant! She absolutely nailed him."

Amber took a step backward and stared at her friends. "Where is he now?"

"No one can say with exact certainty," explained Lily.

"He's in our hearts," smiled Rose.

"We thought you knew," said Frank.

"Now that's an outright lie, Frank Treadwell. How could I possibly know? I wasn't even here. You've done something awful, all of you, and you don't dare tell me. Fraidy cats. But I'll find him. Oh yes I will. I'll go, and search, and find him myself even if it takes me all night. Errrrrrnest!" she called, cupping her hands to her mouth. "It's me, Amber, your friend!" And she ran onto the ice.

"Will somebody tell me what just happened?" asked Max.

"I thought we were talking about Jesus," said Lily.

"We were," Frank agreed. "She wasn't."

Amber crossed the pond, calling, "Errrrrrnest! Ernie old pal! Help is coming! I won't go home until I find you!"

Frank knew better than to run after her. He knew that no one could dissuade Amber from her mission other than Ernest himself, but where was he? The sun hung dangerously close to the treetops. At any moment Amber could veer off into the woods—and into the talons of a hungry owl or a nighthawk! Dear God, he prayed, this is a

horrible misunderstanding. Please, just help us find Ernest and we'll take it from there.

Suddenly he thought of Mr. Chipman and raced over to the General Store. The door banged shut behind him, and Mr. Chipman looked up from his newspaper.

"There's a big mix-up," Frank began. "We have to find Ernest, right away. And then we have to find Amber before she . . . before she . . ." The thought of Amber alone in owl territory was more than Frank could bear. He poured out the story and began to cry.

When he looked up again, he noticed the store phone sitting on the counter. Reaching for it, he dialed. "If Ernest isn't at home, I'm calling the police," he told Mr. Chipman.

"No, wait!" came a thin voice from the back of the store. "Pardon me for listening in, but is it me you're looking for?" Frank spun around and peered into the shadows.

"Ernest! You birdbrain! I've never been so happy to see you in all my life! Get your jacket on. Listen, Amber thinks we knocked you out or something."

"Because of what I did to Rose and Lizbeth?" Frank nodded. "But you guys aren't like that," said Ernest, knotting his scarf.

"Of course we're not," said Frank, pulling him toward the door, "but you're the only one who can convince her of that. Got any flashlights?" Frank called over his shoulder.

"And spare batteries?" asked Ernest, stopping to scan the shelves.

"Never mind the batteries!" thundered Frank. "Go, go!"

❋❋❋❋❋

Later, after they'd found Amber, Ernest admitted that he'd skipped rehearsal so Frank couldn't tease him. "I've been coming to the pond every day before school trying to make myself go out on the ice. But I just can't do it. Ice-skating terrifies me. I knew you'd call me a chicken when you found out, and that's why I didn't come. I'm tired of getting my feelings hurt."

To Frank's surprise, the others spoke up in support of Ernest. They told Frank about times when something he'd said had hurt their feelings, too. "You're caring and you're kindhearted," said Lily, "and we know you'd never hurt a flea, but you're not exactly . . . nice all the time. What you say might be true, but sometimes it's better to say nothing."

In Frank's opinion, everyone should speak the truth all the time. If everyone would just say what they meant and mean what they said, 90 percent of life's misunderstandings would never occur. On the other hand, his habit of speaking candidly had just brought on a near catastrophe. Could he learn to keep his mouth shut? Should he?

❋❋❋❋❋

The children devoted their midweek rehearsal to Scene 4. This was Frank's scene to play Jesus and he wanted to play it straight. No ballet dancer business. No quarterbacking. "I want the characters and the story line to be obvious," he said. "No one in the audience should have to do any guesswork, OK? So let's review. First, the tax collectors and sinners invite me to dinner." Max and Lily nodded.

"While I'm enjoying their company, the hoity-toity religious leaders come snooping around looking for me." Amber and Rose practiced tiptoeing across the ice on their skates. "When you see me hanging out with the town lowlife you assume that I'm just like them." The girls gasped and pointed and made horrified, shame-on-you faces. "When I don't react, you go berserk. Ready, Ernest?"

"Ready, Frank."

Ernest, they had decided, would narrate most of the show since he refused to skate. "Jesus went forthwith unto the house of Levi," Ernest began. "There he dined with despicable sinners: tax collectors, scoundrels, traitors, and thieves . . ."

❋ ❋ ❋ ❋ ❋

"We need more than two despicable sinners and two hoity-toity snoops," Frank said later when they stopped in the General Store to warm up. Max volunteered to recruit some younger children as extras.

"Hey, speaking of extras, did you hear about the foster child?" asked Ernest. "Mrs. Grumble's been talking about a girl somewhere in Hillsborough who needs help."

"Does she need clothes?" asked Lily. "Because I can get her a whole bag full of hideous dresses!" She and Amber looked at each other and broke into the giggles.

"Just sic old Grumbly on the girl and she'll be fit for society in no time," Frank added, but then wondered if he'd sounded mean.

"I know," said Amber. "Let's dedicate 'The Gospel on Ice' to this girl . . ."

"And take up an offering," said Max.

"Or ask for donations," said Rose. "Good ones like sports equipment."

When nobody could think of any reason not to, they agreed that Frank and Amber would meet with Pastor Claire to propose the idea.

13
Positively Molten

Frank was waiting outside Pastor Claire's study when Amber arrived on Saturday morning for their meeting. Pastor Claire answered Frank's knock with a smile. "We're very eager to hear your ideas," she said. Who's we? Frank wondered. He hadn't asked anyone else to come, so he was taken aback to see Mrs. Grumble in the study too.

"Mrs. Grumble called yesterday to see if I knew anything about a foster child living in Hillsborough," explained Pastor Claire. "I figured it must be the same child you'd heard about, Frank, so I suggested that she join our meeting. Now, what do you have in mind?"

"We want to dedicate 'The Gospel on Ice' to this girl—anonymously, of course—and take an offering," said Amber. "Or, if we can find out what she needs, we can ask for donations: school supplies, books, clothes, toys, stuff like that."

"So, what do you think?" Frank asked. Pastor Claire nodded reassuringly, but Mrs. Grumble's mouth hung open in surprise.

"Good heavens!" she exclaimed, giving Amber a horrified look. "You can't dedicate the show to yourself!" Then her voice softened and she patted Amber's arm and said, "Don't worry, dear, we'll find you all the help you need. Anonymously, of course."

Suddenly everything became clear. "Amber, Mrs. Grumble thinks you're a foster child!" Turning to Mrs. Grumble, Frank said, "Now I understand why you wanted to give Amber all those dresses from the Clothing Exchange Box."

"I believe there's been a misunderstanding," Pastor Claire interjected, looking at Mrs. Grumble. "Amber's father is Jake Everly, the new Classics Professor at Hillsborough College. And her mother, Jan Ellis Everly, gives tours at the botanical gardens." As Pastor Claire spoke, Mrs. Grumble turned a sickly shade of green—green as a brussels sprout, thought Frank.

Max, meanwhile, scampered happily along the footpath to Faeron's Pond for rehearsal. They would practice Scene 2 this morning. He was Jesus, and he would perform a miracle. He couldn't wait.

Half an hour later, they were ready for a run-through. While Ernest narrated, Max, Lily, and Rose pantomimed the story of Jesus teaching the crowds from a fishing boat. When Max–as Jesus–had finished teaching, he motioned for the fellow in the next boat–Lily, actually–to pull in his empty fishnet and cast it out again on the other side. Then Rose helped Lily haul the net back to shore, as if it was now full of fish. "Put some muscle into it," Max ordered. "Your net is supposed to be so heavy it floods your boat. And will you at least pretend to be amazed? You're in the middle of a miracle! You should be totally in awe of me."

"Actually, it's Jesus we're in awe of," said Rose.

"Me, Jesus. What's the difference? For five minutes, I am Jesus."

Lily came up with sketch after sketch for the costumes. One week before the show they finally reached a decision: each child would wear a loose-fitting, knee-length tunic with a sash tied at the waist. Lily experimented with different techniques, starting with a loosely knit tunic in the style of a fishnet, but Rose said it was too flimsy, and the audience would never be able to see it. So Lily switched to fabric, and stitched up a silky tunic with fringe. "We'll look graceful no matter how badly we skate," she explained as she modeled it, but the boys refused to wear anything silky, or fringed. She ended up using plain muslin in shades of purple and blue.

Before rehearsal, on Friday, Mrs. Noel took everyone's measurements while Lily assigned colors. Lining up her friends, she slung fabric over their shoulders and squinted and cocked her head and sighed and shook her head and switched it all around until, at last, she felt certain she'd chosen the perfect color for everyone. "Ernest, you are so indigo. Max, you're navy, and Frank, you're a true blue."

For Jesus' costume, Lily had tie-dyed a sheet in red, orange and yellow. "Jesus is spirited and fiery! Don't these colors just erupt with energy?" she exclaimed. "Yes, they do," she answered her own question. "They're positively molten."

※ ❀ ❀ ❀ ❀

Ernest could tell that Max was close to tears. Amber had confronted Max after rehearsal and demanded to know, once and for all, whether there would or would not be scenery for the show. He'd had to admit that the Galilean village he'd promised wasn't going to happen. Normally when Max's bragging came to nothing, Ernest was the first to say, "I told you so." But today he just walked silently along the footpath with his unhappy friend.

"We should've stuck with *Pilgrim's Progress*," Max muttered, after they'd walked all the way to the General Store. Ernest thought about that, and suddenly he had an idea.

Pulling Max into the store, he sat him down, ordered two cocoas, and said, "I just thought of something. When you said we should've stuck with *Pilgrim's Progress,* it dawned on me that that's exactly what we should do! Max, we can have scenery after all, and here's how . . ."

Early the next morning, Ernest and Max were waiting at the clearing when Mr. Rankle drove up. His pickup truck was piled high with scenery from the set of *Pilgrim's Progress*. They examined the scenery, and Ernest helped Max decide what pieces to use, and where. The audience would enter the clearing by the Straight Gate, and exit through the Gates to the Celestial City. Various structures–turned this way and that– became a synagogue, a house, two fishing boats, and a tax collector's booth. Jesus would deliver the Sermon on the Mount from the Hill of Difficulty.

Doubting Castle was the largest piece of scenery, and when Ernest saw it, he told Max not to use it. "Doubt is the enemy of faith. We can't use a castle with that name. Besides, there isn't a castle in my script." But Max couldn't take his eyes off the giant structure, especially when Mr. Rankle hoisted up the turret and fastened it in place.

"I know," cried Max, "you can narrate the show from up there. I can picture the whole thing: from the heights of Doubting Castle, you, Ernest Graves, will tell the world about Jesus Christ. All you need is a megaphone. I'll get you a megaphone. That's one promise I can keep!"

Mr. Rankle was still pounding nails and shimming up corners when Max jogged up with a megaphone, and Dress Rehearsal began.

❋ ❋ ❋ ❋ ❋

Rose dragged Lily out of bed on the morning of the show and led her over to the window. Powdered-sugar snow dusted the landscape. "It's beautiful," Lily yawned, and reached for her sketchbook, but Rose snatched it away.

"Don't sketch it!!! It's not beautiful. Another half inch would mean we can't skate!" Rose paced the floor while Lily got ready. Every few minutes she ran and looked out the window, and she prayed: Dear God, Remember all those times I prayed for snow? Well, I didn't mean today! Please stop the snow before it ruins everything.

The Anniversary Sunday service was duller and lasted longer than usual. Mr. and Mrs. Everly came to church for the first time that morning, and the Noels squeezed together to make room. Cramped and bored, Rose fidgeted the entire time.

During the Anniversary luncheon, she plotted with her friends. "If we don't leave before the speeches begin, we'll be trapped here for another half hour!" When Pastor Theo started for the podium, Rose whispered, "Now!" and off they dashed.

❋ ❋ ❋ ❋ ❋

Amber tugged on Miss Gloria's sleeve. "May I speak with you privately?" she asked. The children were hiding behind a screen of reeds and underbrush while the audience arrived. Miss Gloria bent down on one knee so that she was eye level with Amber.

"This is serious, isn't it?" she said.

Amber nodded. "It's about Scene 5. The Beatitudes. I'm supposed to recite them, but now I can't, I mean, I won't. The problem is I didn't pay attention to their meaning when I memorized them, but I did last night and, Miss Gloria, they're not right."

"Five minutes until show time," Ernest interrupted, pointing to his wristwatch.

Amber's thoughts came tumbling out. "What's 'blessed' about being 'poor in spirit' or

'meek' or 'mournful'? Could this be a mistake?" Amber swallowed hard. "I've been thinking about foster children, Miss Gloria. They leave their homes and move in with kindhearted families, but they probably miss their real parents, even if their real parents weren't good to them, so they must spend a lot of time feeling 'poor in spirit,' and I think that's a tragedy, not a blessing."

"It certainly can be a tragedy," said Miss Gloria, and Amber went on.

"As for 'blessed are the meek,' and 'blessed are you who mourn,' well, let's say you have a friend who's lively, confident, and cheerful. Does that automatically make her . . . I mean, him or her . . ."

" . . . unblessed?" Miss Gloria supplied the very word Amber was looking for.

"Exactly." Amber relaxed a little now that her worries had found words. "And does this . . . um . . . friend have to become a cowardly, wishy-washy mope in order to get God's blessing?"

"No," said Gloria. "God's love and mercy are for everyone."

"So it *is* a mistake," said Amber.

"No," said Miss Gloria.

"Places!" yelled Frank.

Lily pushed Ernest over to Doubting Castle, while Max herded the extras to their starting positions. Rose blazed across the ice like a red-orange comet, but Amber stood fast, as if planted in the frozen ground, and Miss Gloria stayed with her.

Leaning on Every Word

When Pastor Claire reached Faeron's Pond it was already "standing room only"; she'd been lucky to find the last seat next to Jake and Jan Everly, who were anxiously waiting for Amber to skate. "The Gospel on Ice" began with a dazzling performance by Rose as Jesus, skating joyfully while holding the scroll of Isaiah. When the crowds chased her out of the synagogue, she darted past them and vanished in a flash of orange and red.

In Scene 2, Max wore the brightly colored costume and pantomimed the role of Jesus. He matched his movements to every word in the script. While teaching the crowds at the seashore, he stretched his arms out tenderly. During the miracle of the fish, he cupped his hand to his mouth as if calling out instructions. After bidding the fishermen to follow him, he bowed his head and placed his hands over his heart.

Claire applauded enthusiastically after each performance, but she was feeling uneasy. Amber hadn't yet skated, and that didn't seem right. "I expect we'll see her any minute now," she reassured Jan.

But in Scene 3 so many skaters were crammed into one house that even Lily, playing Jesus, was hard to find. Billy Blythe, as the paralyzed man, lay motionless on a toboggan off to the side. Max, Frank, and Rose lifted the toboggan and carried Billy to the house where Jesus was. Instead of lowering him through the roof, the way it happens in the Bible, they delivered Billy to Jesus–toboggan and all–through an open window. As Lily reached down to heal Billy, Claire felt a tap on her shoulder. Hal Louis pointed to a patch of reeds and said, "You're needed."

Claire excused herself and hurried off with Hal. "Amber won't recite the Beatitudes," he explained. "She says they don't make sense." They parted the reeds and came upon Amber as she was showing Gloria a diagram in her notebook.

"See what I'm saying, Miss Gloria? The meaning changes depending on how you read them." Claire asked to look at Amber's diagram.

"You're on to something important," Claire told her. "To understand the Beatitudes we have to think about them from every possible angle. And keep in mind that our Bibles today don't match up word for word with the ancient Greek manuscripts."

"Ancient Greek manuscripts?" Amber's face brightened. "My dad's a classics professor. I can discuss this with him!"

"Perfect," said Claire, "and you'll do Scene 5?"

A round of applause interrupted their conversation. Ernest's voice over the megaphone announced an intermission. Frank, Max, Rose, and Lily charged over to Amber, and Max lit into her. "Billy Blythe played all your parts!! And who told him what to do? I did!! I was so worried; I almost forgot my own parts!"

Even as Amber apologized she was unbowed. "I'm sorry, everybody. What happened is that I learned my lines without thinking about the meaning, and when I finally did, certain things bothered me. And they still do, so I can't do it." She slipped off her tunic and handed it to Max.

"You're backing out on us?" Frank couldn't hide his anger.

"No! I'm not! Listen, we agreed to portray Jesus from our own points of view, but I don't have one. Yet. And I won't go before an audience and pretend that I do!"

Frank was the first to apologize. "Amber, you're right," he said. "We can't ask you to fake it. That would make us hypocrites, and Jesus couldn't stand hypocrites. Our whole next scene is about that. But you can still be in the show, Amber. Why don't you join the crowd? They don't know where they stand either. You can be another extra. An extra extra, get it?" But no one laughed.

"Well, we still need someone to recite the Beatitudes," said Max.

"Where's Ernie?" asked Amber. "He'll do it." But Ernest was nowhere to be seen.

"Uh-oh!" exclaimed Rose. "He's probably stranded in the turret!" She sped off to fill him in on the news, and Claire realized she'd better go too, and find the Everlys.

❄✽❀❁❀

During Scene 4, Max kept an eye on Billy, looked after the extras, and skated his own parts perfectly, but he knew Ernest was going to steal the show. As if narrating from the turret and using the megaphone wasn't special enough, Ernest would now get two turns to be Jesus. He'd be a hero, for sure. Max tried not to feel jealous. Ernest had been unusually kind lately, helping with the scenery and all, but he couldn't skate, and this was a skating show.

During the break between Scenes 4 and 5, Ernest hurried down from the turret and traded costumes with Frank. Now he was Jesus. Frank helped him over to the Hill of Difficulty where he took a deep breath and launched into the Beatitudes. "Blessed are the poor in spirit, for theirs is the kingdom of heaven." His voice quavered at the beginning, but grew steadily stronger. By Scene 6, he'd found his rhythm. "Turn the other cheek," he said. "Go the second mile." The better Ernest got, the worse Max felt. When he couldn't bear it any longer, he turned away and looked up. What?? Even the turret of Doubting Castle appeared to be leaning on Ernest's every word.

Leaning? Oh, no!! Max raced toward the clearing. Mr. Rankle saw him coming and met him at the shoreline, toolbox in hand. They dashed around to the back of the castle to investigate. Mr. Rankle took one look and shuddered. The wedges he'd used to shim up the corners had popped out; the listing castle was in danger of collapsing!

"Whosoever heareth these words of mine, and doeth them, shall be like a wise man, who built his house upon a rock." Ernest's voice, deepened by the megaphone, echoed through an arched window. "The rain fell and the floods came, and the winds blew and beat against that house, but it did not fall, for it was founded upon a rock."

Mr. Rankle shoved a crowbar under the foundation and Max slipped in the wedges. They moved from one section to the next. "Whosoever heareth these words of mine and doeth them not, shall be like a foolish man, who builded his house upon the sand. The rain fell, and the floods came, and the winds blew and beat against the house, and it fell!" roared Ernest.

"That'll do for now," huffed Mr. Rankle.

"And great was the fall of it!"

The audience erupted. Max jumped up and down and waved to get Ernest's attention. "Don't go back up there," he called, pointing to the turret and making an X with his fingers. Ernest nodded. He delivered his closing remarks and then carefully picked his way back down the Hill of Difficulty. As he stepped onto the ice, Max clamped a congratulatory arm around his shoulder. "Thank God you're safe," he whispered. Then he maneuvered Ernest to the center for a group bow, and when the audience chanted, "Author! Author!" Max grinned and launched him back out for a standing ovation.

❄ ❄ ❄ ❄ ❄

Pastor Theo hesitated outside Gloria's classroom. He was reluctant to interrupt the cast party, but he was also fairly certain the children would want to know about Papa Jordan. Slowly he turned the doorknob and stepped inside.

"Bad news," he told them. Papa Jordan had fallen at home and broken his hip.

"Will he be OK? Can we go visit him?" they asked. So Theo made a few phone calls to see what he could arrange.

Mrs. Grumble disapproved. "The last thing an elderly gentleman recuperating from surgery needs is an invasion of noisy children," she told Theo. And what was he thinking when he accepted the Treadwells' offer to drive? What if baby Maeve started wailing or needed a diaper change or spit up on Papa Jordan's bedcovers? Nevertheless, Constance felt a certain pride at having been invited to go along.

Theo and Claire went into the hospital room first, and the others followed when Claire gave the OK signal. Theo cranked up the bed. Papa Jordan looked from face to face, stopping at Max. "You there," he pointed, "aren't you the one who . . .?"

"Yes sir," said Max. "Then you lit the Candle of Hope."

"Two Candles of Hope," Papa Jordan corrected him.

Mrs. Treadwell brought Maeve over to the bed. Papa Jordan played with one of her feet until her satin bootie slipped through his fingertips. "Baa-baa," she gurgled. He smiled, leaned back, and closed his eyes. Theo offered to pray. Lily, who was closest, took one of Papa Jordan's bony hands and curved it gently around her own.

" . . . For thine is the kingdom, and the power, and the glory, forever. Amen." Papa Jordan opened his eyes again and blinked, as if puzzled by the circle of visitors. Then his face softened into something like recognition. "Is this the Celestial City?" he asked.

"I don't know," said Theo. "Is it?"

Papa Jordan held up one hand as if to say, "No, not yet" —or maybe he was waving good-bye. Claire tapped her watch and nodded toward the door. Max, at the foot of the bed, said, "We're with you, Papa Jordan. Come home soon."

"Yes, please try," said Amber.

"We'll be waiting . . ." Frank wiped his eyes with his sleeve as they filed into the hallway.

It was getting late and Constance was about to say so when she noticed Max off by himself looking more forlorn than any of the others. She hesitated for half a second before walking over and giving his shoulders a squeeze. Max didn't pull away. In fact, he looked up at her and said, "Papa Jordan will be OK . . ." His voice wobbled on the word "OK." Was that a statement or a question? Constance couldn't tell.

"Well, he's with God, isn't he?" she replied, as matter-of-factly as she could manage. Max nodded. "So he'll be OK," she continued, "because with God, there is . . ."

"I know." Max closed his eyes. "With God there is hope."

Rose needed a drink of water. Constance accompanied her, and when they returned, Lily approached with a knitting question. Good heavens, she thought, if it wasn't one thing, it was another. "Should I stop here?" Lily asked, showing Constance her work.

"Not necessarily," said Constance. "You've got enough yarn to knit a few more rows. Why not keep going as long as you can?"

On the way home in the car, Frank asked Pastor Theo if there was such a thing as a foster grandparent.

"If there isn't, there ought to be," Pastor Theo replied.

Frank didn't know whether Papa Jordan would want him for a foster grandchild, but he decided he would ask the very next time he had a chance. But would he have a chance? He hoped so. He hoped so, very much. He hoped so very much that he prayed the rest of the way home in the car, and for days to come.

Artist's Notes

In keeping with the illustrations in *Come Worship With Me* (Westminster John Knox Press, 2001), the artwork in this new book is enhanced by the use of Christian symbols. As in that earlier work, design and pattern underscore the theme in each illustration. In *Mouse Tales* Celtic design features more prominently. Initially inspired by the tradition of illuminated manuscripts (e.g., the Book of Kells, 800 AD, and the Lindisfarne Gospels, 710 AD, religious texts embellished with Celtic designs), the Celtic knotwork further emphasized central themes in this book: the concepts of a "beautiful tangle" and the eternal nature of God's creation. The elaborate designs, with their repetitive, interlocking, and interlacing circles and patterns, also offered many opportunities for me to add something of my own quirky understanding or inspiration to this work.

In the very first illustration the scene depicts two of the main characters, Lily and Rose. They are waking in anticipation of the First Sunday of Advent, with hope of the first seasonal snowstorm. The room is symmetrical, with twin beds, flanking a side table. This draws the eye to a triangle of light in the center that implies an unseen participant in the drama. Rose is up first and notices Lily, still asleep, but dreaming. The Celtic knot designs accentuate the complexity that runs throughout these tales. Note the twisted Celtic knot pattern on Rose and Lily's quilts in the first illustration. This particular pattern conjured up images of a double helix strand of DNA, and questions relating to Atoms, Quarks, String Theory, and Creation. With Rose and Lily being twins–this was too irresistible for me to ignore. The design elements in this piece combined to add a new "twist" to the mystery of who, and why, we are.

The final illustration shows Papa Jordan in the hospital with the members of his community literally encircling him. The pattern on his hospital gown is emblematic of the situation as a whole. The pattern: a modified Celtic design of connected circles incorporates the simple yet infinitely complex elements associated with the Circle of Eternity Symbol (identified in the Index of *Come Worship With Me*). The illustration was designed with this theme at its center. Papa Jordan, as the eldest member of his community, is one part within the context of a grander scheme. The others, in reaching toward one another, complete the circle . . . but only with the help and presence of things not seen. The contrasts and eternal truths that lie between life's beginnings and endings are shown through all those present, starting with baby Maeve, the youngest member of the community, and culminating in Papa Jordan.

The first and last illustrations echo one another in structure and theme. Did you notice the similarities between Rose and Lily in their twin beds in anticipation of Advent, and this last illustration? Twin beds remain a constant element, yet a completely different set of circumstances is unfolding around Papa Jordan. Together these illustrations explore the mystery of hope, how it emerges within relationships, when two or more are gathered. The replication of patterns and structure plays with the idea that God really is in the details, and that throughout all the vastness and minutia there are similarities, repetitions, and mutations that play out an infinite number of times in a grand design.

Throughout all these illustrations I have tried to nurture an awareness of the interconnectedness of life, and the wonders of creation. The unique individuals together form a cohesive community–a beautiful tangle of sorts. My hope is that the designs, interwoven with the characters and text, combine to add another dimension to these stories.

Tracey Dahle Carrier

RODENT
REVIEW

Published by Westminster John Knox Press

Vol. 3, No. 4

Nuts
seed
key
mou

New study reveals
reduction in owl
population due to